Dinosaurs

Patricia Walsh

Illustrations by David Westerfield

Heinemann Library
Chicago, Illinois

Customer Service 888-454-2279
Visit our website at www.heinemannraintree.com

Designed by Kimberly Miracle and Q2A Creative
Illustrated by David Westerfield
Photos by Kim Saar, p. 4; Mark Ferry, p. 5
Printed in China by WKT

10 09 08 07 06
10 9 8 7 6 5 4 3 2 1

New edition ISBNs: 1-4034-8923-8 (hardcover)
                   1-4034-8930-0 (paperback)

The Library of Congress has cataloged the first edition as follows:
Walsh, Patricia, 1951-
      Dinosaurs / by Patricia Walsh ; illustrations by David Westerfield.
          p. cm. – (Draw It!)
      Includes bibliographical references and index.
Summary: Presents instructions for drawing twelve different kinds of dinosaurs, including an
Allosaurus, a Stegosaurus, and a Tyrannosaurus.
ISBN 1-57572-349-2 (lib. bdg.)
1. Dinosaurs in art – Juvenile literature. 2. Drawing – Technique – Juvenile literature.
[1. Dinosaurs in art. 2. Drawing – Technique.] I. Westerfield, David, 1956-ill. II. Title.

NC780.5 .W35 2001
743.6– dc21

                                          00025762

Acknowledgments
Cover photograph reproduced with permission of Jim Zuckerman/Corbis.

Every effort has been made to contact copyright holders of any material reproduced
in this book. Any omissions will be rectified in subsequent printings if notice is given
to the publisher.

Some words are shown in bold, **like this**. You can find out
what they mean by looking in the glossary.

Contents

Introduction

Would you like to improve the pictures that you draw? Well, you can! In this book, the artist has drawn pictures of dinosaurs. He has used lines and shapes to draw each picture in small, simple steps. Follow these steps and your picture will come together.

Here is advice from the artist:

- Always draw lightly at first.

- Draw all the shapes and pieces in the right places.

- Pay attention to the spaces between the lines as well as the lines themselves.

- Add details and **shading** to finish your drawing.

- And finally, erase the lines you don't need.

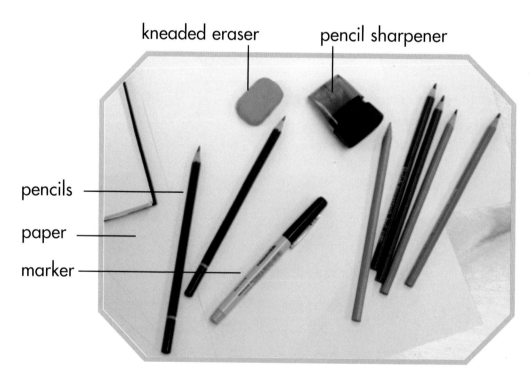

You only need a few supplies to get started.

There are just a few things you need for drawing:

- a pencil (medium or soft). You might also use a fine marker or pen to finish your drawing.

- a pencil sharpener

- paper

- an eraser. A **kneaded eraser** works best. It can be squeezed into small or odd shapes. This eraser can also make pencil lines lighter without erasing them.

Now are you ready? Do you have everything? Then turn the page and let's draw!

The drawings in this book were done by David Westerfield. David started drawing when he was very young. In college, he studied drawing and painting. Now he is a **commercial artist** who owns his own graphic design business. He has two children, and he likes to draw with them. David's advice to anyone who hopes to become an artist is, "Practice, practice, practice—and learn as much as you can from other artists."

Allosaurus

Allosaurus means "different lizard." It got this name because the bones in its back were different from other dinosaurs. The **fossil remains** of this meat-eating dinosaur have been found in Utah.

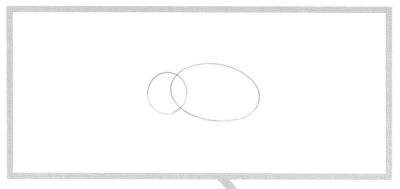

Step 1:
Sketch an overlapping circle and oval.

Step 2:
Sketch a circle for the head. Connect it to the first circle with slightly curved lines for the neck.

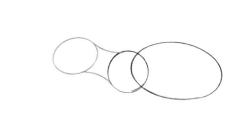

Step 3:
Draw a V on the second circle for the mouth. Draw a straight line under the V for the jaw. Draw a curved line above the V for the **snout**. Make two small, upside-down Vs on top of the head for the bony knobs above the eyes. Add the sweeping, heavy tail. It is wide at the body and narrow at the end.

Step 4:

Use straight lines and small ovals for **guidelines** to make arms and legs. Sketch two short arms under the first circle. The front arm should have two ovals. The back arm should have one. Sketch two long legs under the larger oval. One front leg should have three ovals. The other should have two. Draw a line to smooth out the underside of the body.

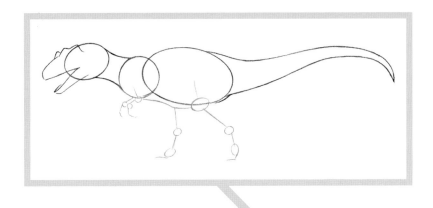

Step 5:

Draw lines on the sides of the ovals to shape the arms and legs. Draw three fingers with claws on each hand and three toes with **talons** on each foot.

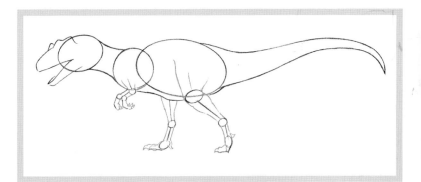

Step 6:

Erase the guidelines. Put an eye under the bony knob on the head. Add a tiny circle on the snout for a nostril. Draw sharp teeth. Add a few wrinkles on the neck. **Shade** in some stripes on the back and some shadows on the legs and stomach.

Ankylosaurus

Ankylosaurus was covered in bony plates set in thick, leathery skin. This covering gave it its name, meaning "stiffened lizard." Ankylosaurus was a plant eater of western North America. It was one of the last dinosaurs to become **extinct**.

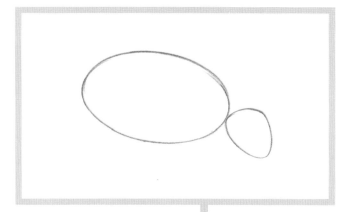

Step 1:

Lightly draw a long oval for the body. Next to the oval, draw a triangle with rounded corners for the head.

Step 2:

Connect the head to the body with two lines. Add the tail by drawing two curved lines that meet in a point.

Step 3:

Begin the four legs with **guidelines**. **Sketch** short, straight lines connected by small ovals. Draw legs on the front side of the dinosaur with three ovals and three short lines. The front leg on the back side has two ovals and three short lines. Draw the back leg on the back of the dinosaur with two short lines and one oval.

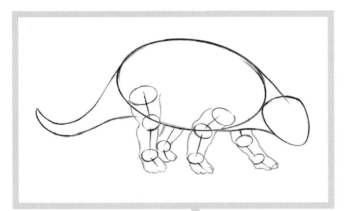

Step 4:

Finish the thick legs with a line on either side of the ovals. Round off the feet. Add toes.

Step 5:

Draw two triangular spikes near the top of the head. Add another one on the neck, on the left side of the head. Draw a dark circle for the eye. Draw two slanted lines on the **snout** for the nostrils and a line for the mouth. Erase the guidelines. Draw one curvy line along the side of the body. Add several curved lines across the back and tail.

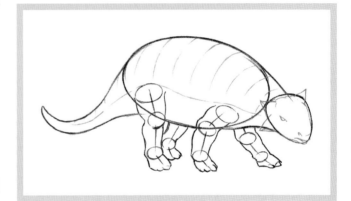

Step 6:

Draw rows of triangles to add spikes to the back and tail. Make the end of the tail round. **Shade** the underside of the body and under the feet.

Brachiosaurus

The name Brachiosaurus means "arm lizard." Its name refers to this dinosaur's long front legs. It stood taller than a four-story building. Brachiosaurus was a plant eater whose **remains** have been found in the western United States, Africa, and Europe.

Step 1:

Start with a circle. Then **sketch** two ovals that overlap it. These are the **guidelines** for the body.

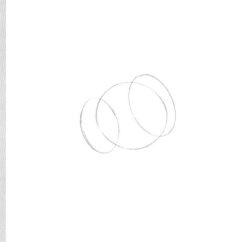

Step 2:

Draw a small oval high above the body for the head. Draw two long S curves to connect the head to the body and make the neck. On the left side, draw a tail that begins as wide as the oval and that ends in a point.

Step 3:

Smooth the guidelines along the back with a bold line. Begin the four legs with straight guidelines and circles at the knees and ankles.

Step 4:

Shape each thick leg with a line on either side of the circles. Square off the feet. Draw a line to smooth out the underside of the body.

Step 5:

Add a bump to the top of the head. Put a dot in the bump for the nostril. Near the top of the head, add a dot for the eye that can be seen in this picture. Halfway down the head, draw a short line to make the **snout**. Near the bottom of the head draw a longer line for the mouth. Erase the guidelines.

Step 6:

Finish by adding light, short wrinkle lines for the dinosaur's skin. **Shade** in the underside of the tail and body, and the neck under the head. Use the side of the pencil lead to make a shadow on the ground under this giant dinosaur.

Iguanodon

Iguanodon's name means "iguana tooth." Its teeth looked like a modern iguana lizard's teeth. This dinosaur has been found on every continent except Antarctica.

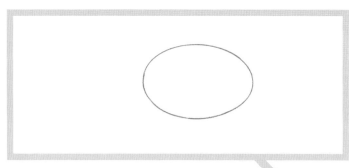

Step 1:

Sketch an oval for the body.

Step 2:

Add a small circle slightly above and to the side of the oval. Connect these two shapes with a curved line below and a U-shaped line above. Add the sideways V-shaped tail to the oval.

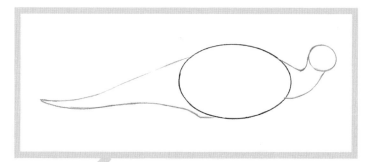

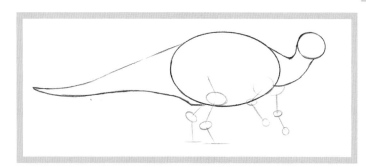

Step 3:

Begin the four legs with short, straight **guidelines**. Draw small ovals for the knees, ankles, and shoulders. The front legs should both have three ovals. The near back leg should have two ovals, and the far back leg should have one. Draw a straight line under each of the back legs.

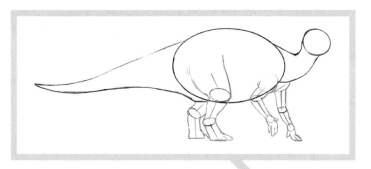

Step 4:

Draw a line on either side of the ovals to make thick back legs and thin front arms. Add toes to each back foot. Add fingers to the end of each arm.

Step 5:

To finish the head, change the shape of the circle by adding a **snout** with a U-shaped notch for the mouth. Make a dot for the nostril. Draw a small oval for the eye. Add short curved lines above and below the eye. Add two short curved lines where the head meets the neck.

Step 6:

Erase guidelines. **Shade** the underside. Draw the ground under this dinosaur by making a few pencil strokes. Add some squiggly lines to show bushes.

Parasauralophus

Parasauralophus was a duck-billed dinosaur. It had a hollow tube on its head about as long as a kitchen table. Its name means "similar **crested** lizard." This dinosaur has been found in the western part of the United States and Canada.

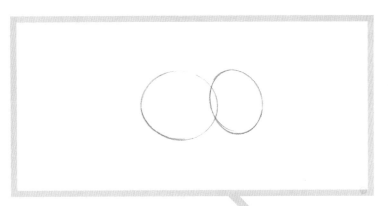

Step 1:

Start the body by **sketching** a circle. Draw an oval that overlaps the circle's right side.

Step 2:

Sketch a small oval for the head. Connect the head to the body with U-shaped lines on top and bottom. Smooth the back and underside with sweeping lines. Continue these two lines to a point to make the tail.

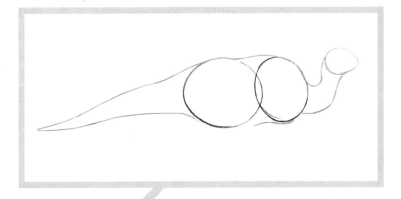

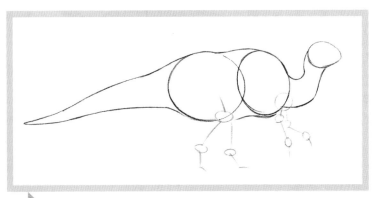

Step 3:

Sketch short **guidelines** to begin the legs. Draw small ovals for the knees and ankles. Use short, straight lines to show the feet and toes.

Step 4:

Draw a line on either side of the ovals to shape the legs. Add two toes to the back feet. Add webbed hands, like duck feet, to the front legs.

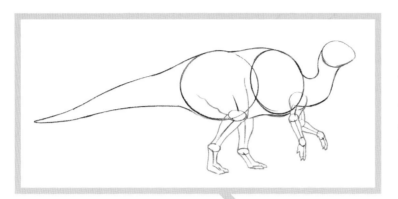

Step 5:

Add a long tube with a circle at the end to the back of the head. Draw a rounded bill on the front. Add a dark circle on the head, for an eye. Make a V on the bill for the mouth. Put a dot for the nostril above it, near the top edge of the bill.

Step 6:

Erase the guidelines. **Shade** the underside of the dinosaur. Make a shadow on the ground by using the side of the pencil lead.

Pteranodon

Pteranodon means "winged and toothless." It was not a dinosaur, but a flying reptile that may have glided rather than flown. It had huge wings and a turkey-sized body. **Fossils** of Pteranodon have been found in Kansas.

Step 1:

Begin by drawing a straight line. Then draw two simple shapes along the line—a triangle at the top and an oval midway down. The triangle will be the head, and the oval will be the body.

Step 2:

Draw two lines to connect the triangle and the oval. This will be the neck. **Sketch** four long, curved lines that begin at the straight line above and below the oval.

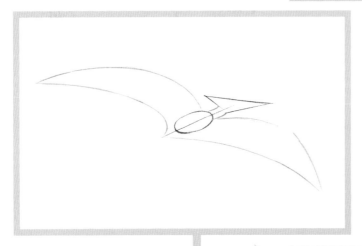

Step 3:

Draw two small circles on the oval body for shoulders. Then draw the wing arms in three pieces. They look like zigzag lines. Add three fingers at the end of each arm.

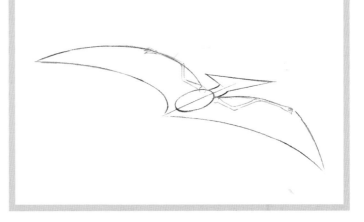

Step 4:

Draw a sharp V under the triangle head to make the lower beak. Extend and round off the top point of the triangle to make the **crest**. Add a dot for an eye on the top of the head, near the crest, and a tiny curved line for a nostril to the right of the eye, on the beak.

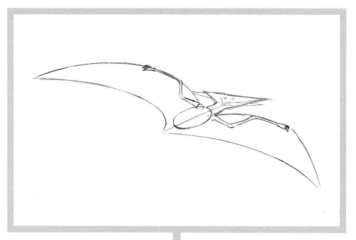

Step 5:

Draw each leg in two parts. Draw a small circle at the knee. Add the back feet. Make the tail by darkening the lines that form the center point of the wings.

Step 6:

Erase the **guidelines** and darken the outlines. **Shade** the wings and body. Sketch loops for clouds to show the Pteranodon soaring in the sky.

Spinosaurus

Spinosaurus means "spiny lizard." This meat-eating dinosaur had tall spines on its back. The spines supported a fin that may have controlled its body temperature. **Remains** of Spinosaurus were found in North Africa.

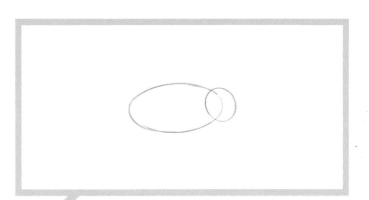

Step 1:

Sketch a long oval. Make a smaller oval that overlaps one end of the first oval.

Step 2:

Draw a circle above and to one side for the head. Attach the circle to the oval with two curved lines. Sketch a sideways W on the side of the head for the **snout**. The top of the W should be a little wider than the bottom.

Step 3:

Draw the tail so it is as wide as the end of the oval and narrows to a point. Sketch a curved **guideline** above the body for the fin. Begin the short front legs with short guidelines connected by circles. Sketch the back legs as three lines connected with circles for the hips, knees, and ankles.

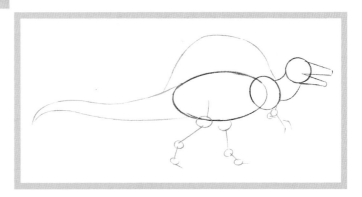

Step 4:

Make the line for the belly bolder. Shape the legs by drawing a line on either side of the circles. Add two toes to the back legs and pointy, clawlike hands to the front legs.

Step 5:

Add two tiny upside down Vs on top of the head. Draw an eye under the closest small V. Add a circle for the nostril near the point of the snout. Add two rows of sharp teeth. Make the fin guideline wavy and bold.

Step 6:

Erase guidelines. Darken the outlines. Sketch **vertical** lines on the fin. **Shade** in the top part of the Spinosaurus. Add spots of color on top of the body. Use the side of the pencil lead to add a patch of shadow under the dinosaur's body.

Stegosaurus

The plates on its back gave Stegosaurus a name that means "plated lizard." The larger plates were a little longer and wider than a computer monitor. This dinosaur has been found in what is now Colorado, Utah, and Wyoming, and in parts of Europe.

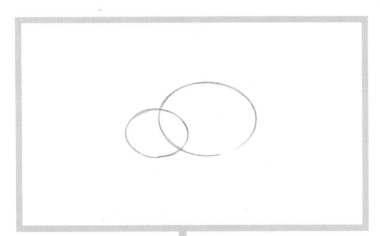

Step 1:

Begin by drawing two overlapping ovals. Make the one on the left smaller than the other oval.

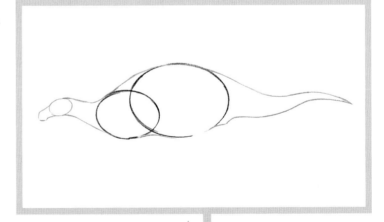

Step 2:

Sketch a small oval for the head to the left of the smaller oval. Then connect the three shapes with a long sweeping outline on the top and bottom. Continue the lines to make a rounded **snout** in front and a pointed tail in the back.

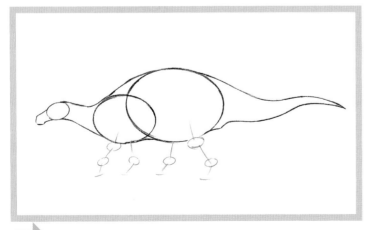

Step 3:

Use straight **guidelines** joined by ovals at the knees and ankles to begin the four legs. Add lines underneath each guideline to be the feet.

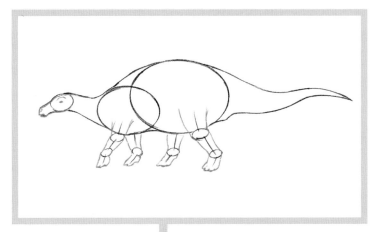

Step 4:

Draw a line on either side of the ovals to shape thick, short legs. Make the lines of the head smoother. Make the line at the bottom of the snout thicker to show a mouth. Add dots for an eye and a nostril.

Step 5:

Draw two rows of diamond-shaped plates along the back. Draw four spikes at the end of the tail.

Step 6:

Add up-and-down pencil strokes to the plates. Darken the top and underside of the body. **Shade** in a shadow underneath the dinosaur's body.

Triceratops

Triceratops had three horns. Its name means "three-horned face." These dinosaurs once roamed western North America. They were among the last dinosaurs to become **extinct**.

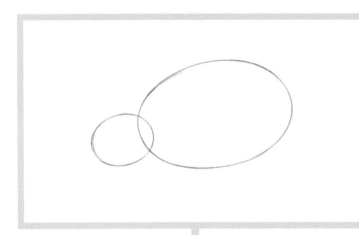

Step 1:

Sketch two overlapping ovals. The right one should be big, and the left one should be small.

Step 2:

Start the four legs with short, light **guidelines**. Draw ovals for the shoulder, hip, knees, and ankles. Add curved lines at the ends for feet.

Step 3:

Draw a line on either side of the ovals to make thick, short legs. Add the tail. It starts wide and ends in a point.

Step 4:

On the head, sketch a beaklike **snout**. Add a line that curves from the bottom of the beak up into the head. This is the jaw. Behind the head, sketch a circle for the **frill**. Draw a curved line to connect the frill to the head. Connect the bottom of the snout to the chest with one bold line.

Step 5:

Draw a small triangular horn on top of the snout. Add a dot for the nostril under the horn. Add two squiggly lines through the snout near the tip. Add a dark oval for the eye and curved lines above and below it. Draw two long, curved, pointed horns on top of the head. Erase the guidelines.

Step 6:

Add little bumps along the edge of the frill and the spine. **Shade** the underside of the dinosaur, and shade a shadow on the ground underneath.

Tyrannosaurus

This huge, meat-eating dinosaur was given the name Tyrannosaurus, which means "**tyrant** lizard." **Fossils** of Tyrannosaurus have been found in Montana, Wyoming, and South Dakota.

Step 1:

Draw a circle with a smaller oval overlapping it on the right. This will start the body.

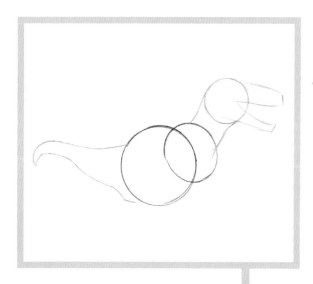

Step 2:

Draw a circle above and to the right side for the head. Connect the head to the body with two lines. Add a big sideways M on the right side of the head to make the **snout**. Draw the tail next. It is thick near the body and pointed at the tip.

Step 3:

Sketch guidelines for two long legs in the back and two small legs in the front. Sketch three larger circles on the lines for the back legs. Sketch three smaller circles on the near front leg and two small circles on the far front leg.

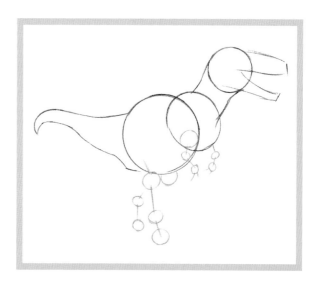

Step 4:

Draw a line on either side of the circles to shape the legs. Draw three long **talons** on the back feet. Draw two strong claws on the front feet.

Step 5:

Shape the snout by adding two bumps to the top. Add a circle for the eye under the first bump. Line the inside of the jaws with sharp teeth. Darken the outline of the head, tail, and body.

Step 6:

Erase the guidelines. Add **shading** to the underside of the dinosaur. Use the side of the pencil lead to add soft lines for the ground.

Velociraptor

Velociraptor means "swift robber." This dinosaur got this name because of its speed and grasping hands. It was a fierce meat eater about the size of an adult human. Fossils of Velociraptor have been found in **Mongolia**, China, and Russia.

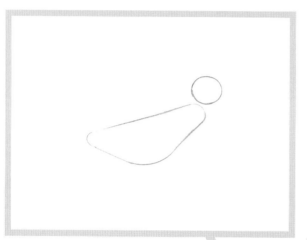

Step 1:

Sketch a triangle with rounded corners to begin the body. Add a circle to the top corner for the head.

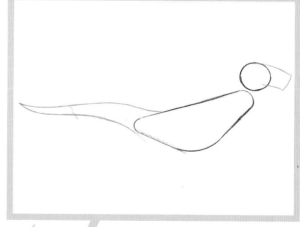

Step 2:

Draw a rectangle on the right side of the circle for a **snout**. On the left corner of the triangle, draw two sweeping lines that end in a point for the tail.

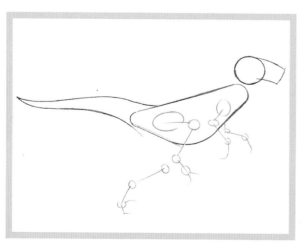

Step 3:

Draw four ovals, two big and two small, on the body. These are the hip, shoulder, elbow, and knee. Sketch **guidelines** for the legs. Each leg has three line segments. Draw three small ovals along each back leg and two on each front leg.

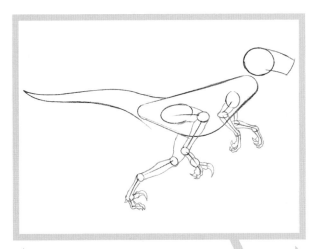

Step 4:

Draw lines on either side of the ovals to shape short front legs and long back legs. Add three long fingers at the end of each front leg and three pointed **talons** to each foot.

Step 5:

Shape the head with a long sideways V to make the mouth. Make the top line of the snout more curved, and put a bump on the top. Add an eye under the bump. Add many sharp teeth. Draw a backward C for a nostril. Make the lines for the body smoother and bolder.

Step 6:

Draw a row of little Vs along the back. **Shade** the Vs and the underside of the dinosaur. Use a few pencil strokes to make the ground beneath the Velociraptor's powerful feet. Draw some squiggly lines to show bushes.

Glossary

commercial artist person who designs and illustrates things for other people

crest bony bump on the head. Crests of dinosaurs ranged in size from small bumps to very long tubes.

extinct no longer alive

fossil trace of an animal or plant that has been preserved in stone

frill bony shield covering the neck

Mongolia region in Asia that includes part of northern China

remains what is left of a dead body

snout part of an animal's head that includes the nose, mouth, and jaws

talon claw of an animal that eats other animals or insects

tyrant someone or something that uses power in a cruel way

Pronunciation Guide

Allosaurus – AL-o-sawr-us

Ankylosaurus – ang-KYL-o-sawr-us

Brachiosaurus – BRAK-ee-o-sawr-us

Iguanodon – ig-WAHN-o-don

Ornithomimus – or-nith-o-MY-mus

Parasauralophus – par-ah-sawr-OL-o-fus

Pteranodon – tayr-AN-o-don

Spinosaurus – SPY-no-sawr-us

Stegosaurus – STEG-o-sawr-us

Triceratops – try-SAYR-ah-tops

Tyrannosaurus – ty-RAN-o-sawr-us

Velociraptor – veh-loss-ih-RAP-tor

Art Glossary

guideline
light line used to shape a drawing. This line is usually erased in the final drawing.

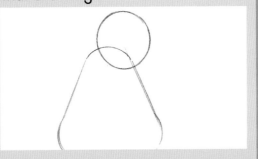

kneaded eraser
soft, squeezable eraser used to soften dark pencil lines

shade
make darker than the rest

sketch
draw quickly and roughly

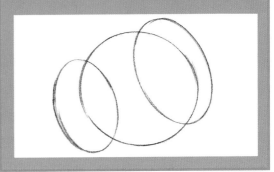

vertical
line that is straight up and down

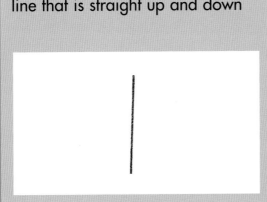

Find Out More

Books

Court, Rob. *How to Draw Dinosaurs*. Eden Prairie, Minn.
  Child's World, 2005.

Murawski, Laura. *How to Draw Dinosaurs*. New York: PowerKids Press, 2001.

Oxlade, Chris. *The Mystery of the Death of the Dinosaurs*. Chicago:
  Heinemann Library, 2002.

Quigley, Mary. *Dinosaur Digs*. Chicago: Heinemann Library, 2006.

Websites

The Field Museum - Sue
http://www.fieldmuseum.org/sue/index.html

Index